Police Car ABC's

Wendy Schoolmeester
Illustrated by: Tiffany Marie Koob

AuthorHouse™
1663 Liberty Drive
Bloomington, IN 47403
www.authorhouse.com
Phone: 833-262-8899

Because of the dynamic nature of the Internet, any web addresses or links contained in this book may have changed
since publication and may no longer be valid. The views expressed in this work are solely those of the author and do
not necessarily reflect the views of the publisher, and the publisher hereby disclaims any responsibility for them.

Any people depicted in stock imagery provided by Getty Images are models,
and such images are being used for illustrative purposes only.
Certain stock imagery © Getty Images.

This book is printed on acid-free paper.

ISBN: 978-1-4389-6276-4 (sc)

Library of Congress Control Number: 2009902220

Print information available on the last page.

Published by AuthorHouse 03/14/2022

authorHOUSE®

Respectfully dedicated to the law enforcement community, particularly Sergeant Jeff, Trooper Laurie, and Deputy Mike. Thank you! ~WCS

For my amazing daughter, Haylee Marie. ~TMK

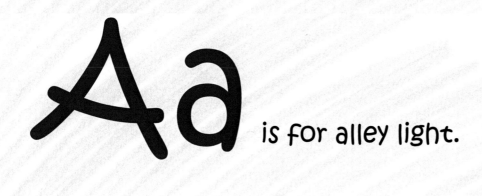 is for alley light.

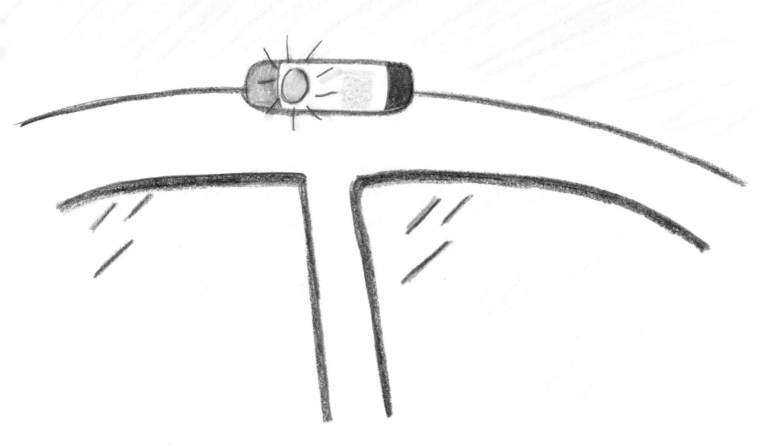

An alley light is on the side of the light bar on top of the police car.
Officers use it to light up dark places.

Bb is for broom.

A broom is used to sweep up the mess after a car accident.

Cc is for computer.

A computer is used for checking on a driver's license and license plate number. Traffic tickets can be printed from the computer.

Dd

is for dogcatching pole.

The dogcatching pole is used for rescuing and restraining stray dogs.

Ee

is for emergency lights.

Red and blue emergency lights warn others to slow down or to pull over and stop. It is a warning that can be seen.

Ff
is for flare.

An officer will use a road flare at night to caution others to approach slowly because an obstacle may be in their way.

Gg is for GPS.

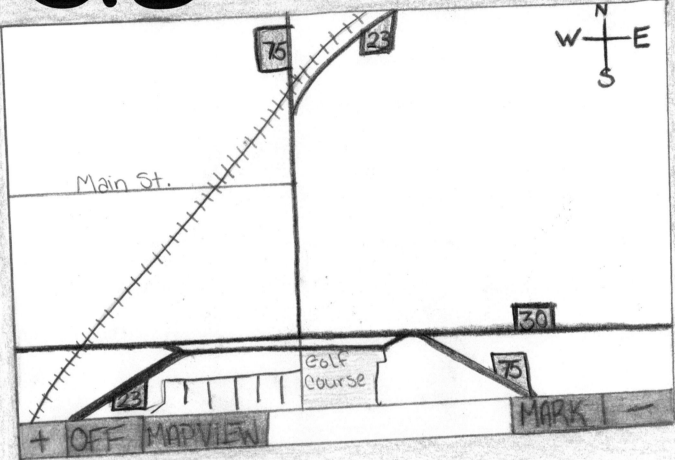

A GPS, or Global Positioning System device, can be used by the officer to locate someone who's lost or by dispatch to locate the police car when it is in an emergency situation.

Hh 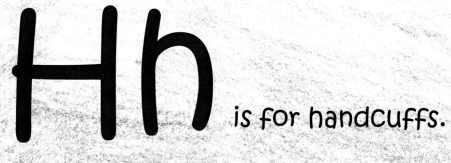 is for handcuffs.

Handcuffs secure a person's wrists together. They help prevent criminals from escaping.

Ii is for information sheet.

Information Exchange Sheet

Accident Information

Date	Day of Week	Time	Investigation at Scene by Security	No. of Vehicles	Was there an Injury	Was there a death	Patrolman
			Yes No		Yes No	Yes No	

Street Name _____   At Intersection With/or _____   Feet   N E / S W of Street Name

Vehicle #1

Driver's Name (Last, First, Middle)			

Address (No. & Street)		Phone No.

City		State	Zip Code

D.O.B.	Sex	D.L #		State

Vehicle owner's Name

Address	Phone #

City	State	Zip Code

Decal	Color	Command

License plate	State	Make	Year	Type

Insurance Co. Agent/phone Number

Insurance Policy Number

Vehicle #2

Driver's Name (Last, First, Middle)			

Address (No. & Street)		Phone No.

City		State	Zip Code

D.O.B.	Sex	D.L #		State

Vehicle owner's Name

Address	Phone #

City	State	Zip Code

Decal	Color	Command

License plate	State	Make	Year	Type

Insurance Co. Agent/phone Number

Insurance Policy Number

After two cars have collided, an information sheet is filled out by the officer. Everything that happened is written on the sheet, and a copy is given to each driver so both have each other's stories.

Jj is for jacket.

The jacket will keep the officer warm and dry in cold, wet weather.

Kk

is for Kevlar vest.

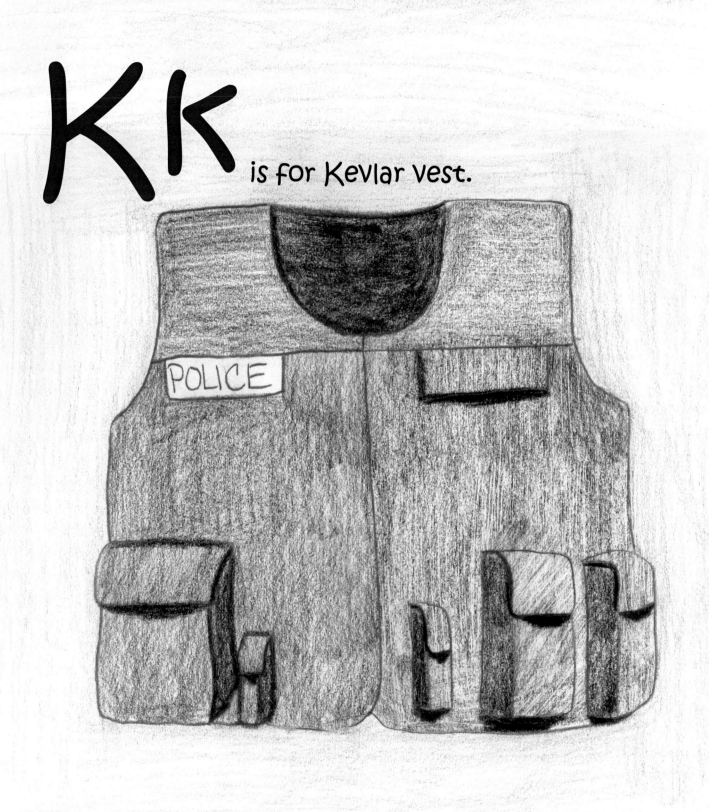

POLICE

Kevlar vest is another name for bulletproof vest. It is called Kevlar because that is the material the vest is made from.

Ll is for latex-free gloves.

Latex-free gloves are put on the hands for protection against germs that are found in body fluids like blood and saliva.

Mm is for microphone.

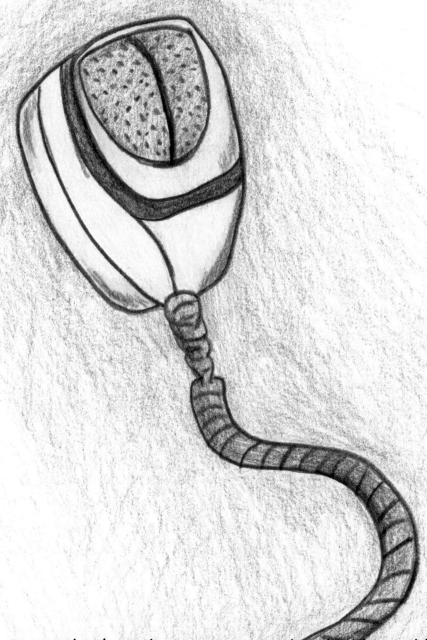

A microphone attached to the camera on the dashboard is used for recording all sounds that happen in front of the police car. The recording could be used as evidence in court.

Nn
is for name tag.

The name tag is for identifying the officer who is on duty.

 is for oxygen tank.

An oxygen tank is used when someone is having a hard time breathing or for heart attack victims.

Pp is for pocket mask.

A pocket mask is used to deliver air to a person who is not breathing. The pocket mask will keep the officer safe from germs.

Qq is for quilt.

The quilt is used to keep accident victims warm while they wait for an ambulance.

Rr

is for radar gun.

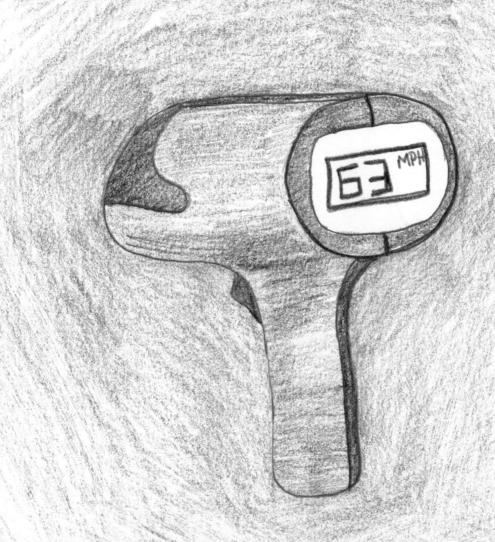

A radar gun can be handheld or mounted on the police car. It is used to detect the speed of an approaching vehicle.

Ss is for siren.

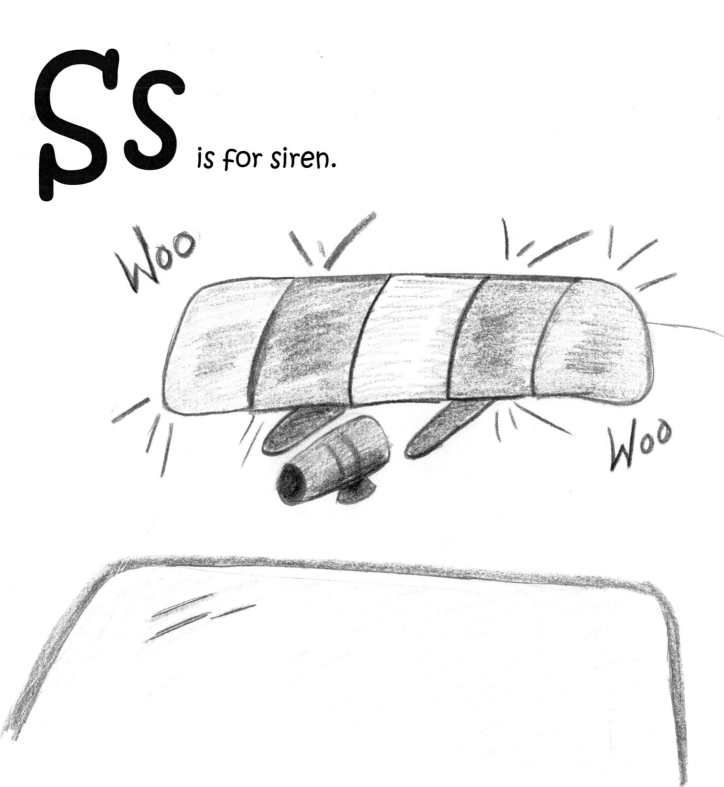

A siren will alert others to the approaching police car before it is seen. The siren cautions others to be careful. It is a warning that can be heard.

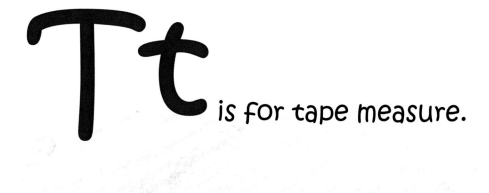

Tt is for tape measure.

A tape measure is used for measuring skid marks from tires to figure out how fast a car had been going before it crashed.

Uu is for unlock waiver.

Unlock Waiver

ICR#_____

I, the undersigned, as the person in lawful control of the vehicle Liscense #_____ do hereby release the City of_____ the City Police Department and any of their Agents from any Liability for damages that may arise from the unlocking or attempted unlocking of the above mentioned Vehicle on the _____ day of _____ 20___.

_____
Signature

_____
Date

I, hereby acknowledge receipt of payment for sum of $30.00.

_____
Signature of Officer

_____   _____
Cash   Check #

The officer will have an unlock waiver form signed by people who have locked their keys in their car. The form states the officer is not responsible for any damage caused to the car in unlocking it.

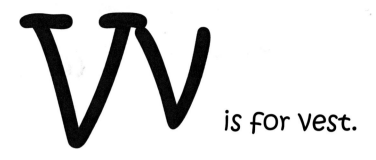 is for vest.

A vest is worn when an officer is directing traffic, and it is very reflective so the officer can easily be seen and kept safe.

Ww is for weapons.

Weapons are only used when needed for protection. A weapon can be a baton, gun, or Taser.

Xx is for EXcel spreadsheet.

	□ X

File | Edit | View | Format | Tools | Date | Window | Help

	E	F	G	H	I	J
3	Crime Categories by Attempted/Completed					
4						
5						
6		Count of Incident	Attempt			
7		Offense	A		C	GrandTotal
		11A			8	8
8		11B			1	1
9		11D			2	2
10		12D	1		9	10
11		13A			30	30
12		13B			171	171
13		200			4	4
14		220	5		58	63
15		23C			92	92
16		23D			5	5
17		23E			40	40
18		23F			57	50
19		23G			205	205
20		23H			31	31
21		240	1		25	26
22		250			2	2
23		270			181	181
24		290			61	61
25		35A			6	6
26		40A			10	10
27		520				
28		GrandTotal	8		1005	1013
29						

Officers do paperwork in their police car. Their car becomes their office. The Excel spreadsheet is used for keeping track of all duties performed by the officer throughout the day.

Yy is for yellow tire marker.

The yellow tire marker is like a crayon used to smudge tires on cars that are parked illegally. The officer can tell by the mark if the car has been moved or not.

Zz is for Z-tool.

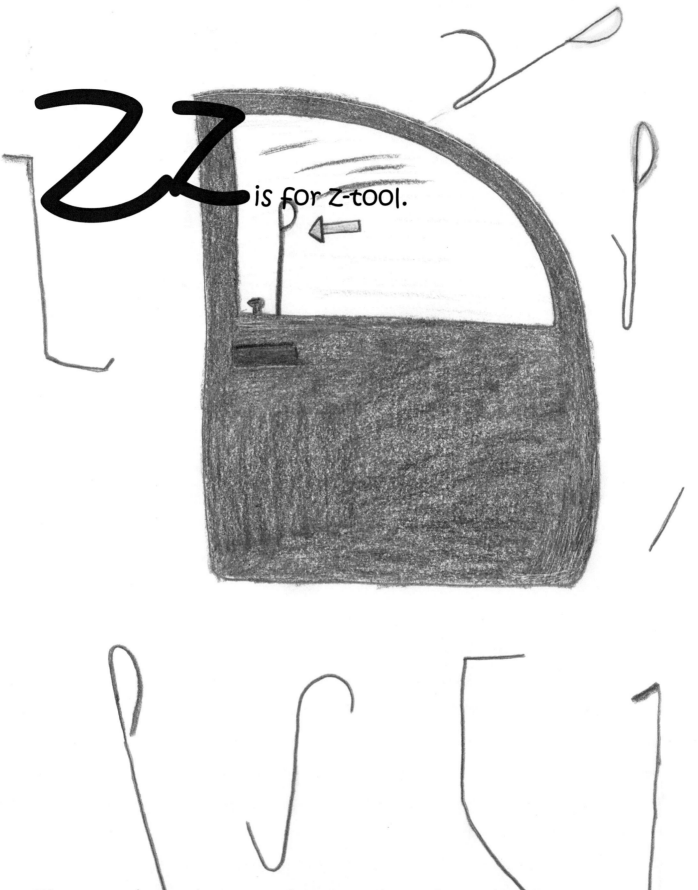

The z-tool is used for opening locked car doors. It can open almost all car doors made from the 1950s to the present.

Printed in the United States
by Baker & Taylor Publisher Services